a rarity

Mattie Paige

Mattie Paige

Contents

a rarity

For anyone told they wouldn't make it to 18 years old.

You're not alone and I see you.

Mattie Paige

a rarity

Warnings

This book contains sensitive material that may be disturbing to some readers. Discretion is advised for the following content warnings:

- Foul language
- Mentions of death and thoughts of death
- References to medical trauma (nothing on page)
- References to the hardships of having a chronic illness
- Negative thoughts, attitudes, and beliefs concerning one's own body and self-worth

This book also contains content that may be encouraging to some readers, such as:

- Acceptance and acknowledgement of the pain of a rare disease/chronic illness
- A touch of gratitude
- Ending with hope

A Word from the Author

Dear reader,

Whether you skim, deep dive or annotate, I appreciate your support. This collection is the most meaningful thing I have ever written and will likely remain that way for a long time. It is a vulnerable story based on my life with Cystic Fibrosis (CF), and is meant to shed light on the circumstances people with chronic illnesses may experience or relate to, particularly those with CF.

"a rarity" allows all the awful, wretched aspects of having a rare disease to exist alongside the beautiful, lovely things of life. Admittedly, it took me a while to feel like acceptance could even be possible. This book is my attempt to move further along the acceptance continuum.

"a rarity" starts with me processing my childhood while wondering why my friends did not face the same medical situations I did. The second part describes my adolescent years trying to understand my body and advocate for myself. The third installment navigates early adulthood, my current life stage. The fourth, and final, part dives into the emotions I find comfort in, the silver linings of my life, and the thoughts and beliefs that help me cope.

Whether or not you have a rare disease or chronic illness, I hope you view this book as an opportunity to learn about someone whose life may, or may not, look like yours. Ideally, this collection will encourage conversations that move society forward in its empathy, compassion and inclusiveness.

Thank you again for giving my life struggles meaning by reading this collection. I'll see you on the next page. <3

Sincerely,
Mattie Paige

Mattie Paige

Prologue: My Child

Such a petite girl.
Has the weight of the world,
From shots and scars galore.
I hope you still feel my adore.

Oh, my child,
I love you so much.
I'm so sorry for your bad luck,
Your stomach had an obstruct.

Oh, my child,
So fragile.
Tied with wires.
How could you have something so dire?

Oh, my child,
Cuddled in the NICU.
Finger holds, just for you.
I'll still be here,

No matter the fear.

Part One: Childhood Memories

Applesauce & M&Ms

1, 2, 3
Applesauce please!
A, B, C,
Can you swallow this please?

The enzymes get popped open,
To pour into my snack.
Applesauce is perfect,
For a late night pact.

A mini-M&M to swallow,
A practice for tomorrow.
Pills will come soon,
But for now, I'll give you a spoon!

Rewards

I get a sticker
For putting up
With that squeezing cuff.

I get a lollipop
For coughing up
Mucus for that cup.

I get a high-five
For seeing that new guy
The doctors swore by.

I get a fun lunch
For letting the needle lady
Take from my red blood.

I get lots of rewards
For sticking through
Medical visit hordes.

Treatment Time

It's really very hard
To sit still for so long.
To take my six-year-old energy,
And turn it into compliance.

My parents tried their best,
To make it as fun as possible.
To carve out a routine,
Filled with intriguing new things.

My favorite treatment time memory,
Is not one I actually remember.
It's based on this faded old picture
My parents pull from a dusty binder.

I have my favorite doll,
Wearing an inhalation mask,
Strapped to her head,
Her body in my dimpled hands

I make her wait.
The agonizing twenty minutes.
We breathe deep together.
We are feeling better.

22

We Still Play

We have a mind,
We have a heart,
We like to make art!

We trace our letters,
And subtract from numbers,
We even like timely slumbers!

A colorful kitchen,
A hearty tinman,
We like to play all day!

I cough more than you,
And miss school,
Because I feel blue.

When I see you soon,
We'll pretend to survive,
The deep blue!

I may be different,
Or so my adults say,
But to me it's a good day,
Because we still play!

24

The Nurse is My Friend

I see her every day.
Around the clock and before I play.
She talks about my stay,
While I wonder if she checks everyone's airway.

Lunch comes around midday,
My parents, I must obey.
I skip to my friends doorway,
So she can feed me pills straightaway.

I never thought I'd make
A friend in this adult.
She asks me my thoughts,
I'm happy someone understands my lot.

She's quite good at pretend,
And keeping track of how to tend.
She even has a nebulizer to lend.
This is why I say, the nurse is my friend.

We'll Make It Work

An invite pinned to the fridge.
Next to the drawing of my vest,
My dearest friend turns 10.
Can I please, *please* attend?

I promise to take my pills,
With each forkful of food.
And to listen to my body
If my breath, I lose.

"I'm sorry it's not so simple,
You're so young and brittle.
It's not a punishment.
Yet, you need your regiment.

I'm not sure you're old enough,
With your precious medical stuff.
To endure an overnight.
Do I trust others to treat my child right?

I want this for you too,
I really do trust you.
I'm just so concerned...
But we'll make it work."

Treatments before drop off,
Pills explained to the adult.
You get your fill of fun,
Until the rising sun

Why do you not take pills?

The pills are my normal,
And my coughs my comfort.
I thought it would be yours too?

I leave for school,
Taking inhalers for fuel.
Did your mom talk to your teacher too?

Down paper covered halls,
To the lunchroom we fall.
Did you stop by the nurse before this talk?

All of these questions flood my mind,
As I learn, we all live different lives.

Why do you not take pills before you eat?
How can you just so easily breathe?

How odd that we are not the same,
And you live a totally different way.

Part Two: Growing Pains

Their Bodies That Work

Their lungs pull air in.
Their hearts pump blood out.
Their limbs have all their ends.
Their brains have all their wits.

Their bodies that work,
Pull from genes that don't twist,
And experiences that don't pluck
The privilege from their annoyingly good luck.

Dichotomy

Just because I'm in high spirits,
Doesn't mean my body isn't in a low place.

Our Advocacy Color: Purple

One of my favorite family traditions is attending the CF Walk. When I was younger, it was just good fun. For some reason, people paid great attention to me on that day. I always got a free, purple t-shirt from the hosts. And the vendors had tubs of bananas, sodas, donuts and salty snacks—all free.

Looking back, the creators of the fundraisers knew their audience.

I didn't grow up knowing the cause of my family's advocacy. Why everyone fundraised in my honor, months in advance, for what seemed like one, dreadfully early morning. Why we drove an hour away, just to walk for what felt like hours while donning matching shirts.

Of course, my parents did a phenomenal job explaining the "why's", but it didn't click until I was older.

I didn't know that the free shirt I got every year was a signal to other CF'ers. A purple cotton sign to stay at least six-feet-apart so we don't spread infections.

I didn't know we needed more research. I didn't know funding wasn't a given. That it was up to those who cared about the efforts to finance it.

And my people cared.

My grandma's best friend consistently split her donation between my sister and I, so we couldn't argue over who raised more.

My friends and I performed our choreographed jump rope routine after all that walking, just because it was fun and they came to support.

My brother even came down while he was away at college.

It wasn't about the money. Well, not entirely.

It was about making memories. About dripping sweat and growing smiles as the group of us crossed the finish line, yelling in glee. Each step our team took was another piece of evidence that people cared about me and my disease.

And I love those memories. I do.

But I also feel somber. Nostalgic.

Missing the days before I knew how permeating this disease is. Longing for the times before I knew what "progressive disease" felt like.

Back then, I could at least pretend I was like other kids. The way I ran around, played and lived life in multiple colors, not just purple.

Now, I don't think I could pretend, even if I wanted to. Which I don't.

It's too stressful to pretend to be something you're not.

And I'm tired of showing up like anyone other than who I am.

It's just weird that even the happiest of memories have a stroke of disease in them.

Flat Soda

If I was
As I was supposed to be,
I'd be a dark liquid,
In a glass.
Fizzing with bubbles,
And beloved by the class.

Pop the top off,
I'd have enough energy,
To spew out,
And have enough left,
To refresh.
I wish I couldn't contest.

I was left out too long,
My bubbles turned flat.
After this day I had
I can't wait to be,
Poured out.
On the concrete.

Pluto Is A Planet

Just because I don't meet your criteria,
Doesn't mean we're not worth the same.
I am the smallest of planets,
But the greatest of names.

You outcasted me
Because I'm not the same size.
For a while I focused on,
Your system more than mine.

It made me feel blue.
That I couldn't be with you.
I cried during my orbit,
But my tears never reached you.

The oddest of blessings,
When my tears froze on Eris.
We became fast friends,
Through our slower paces.

We have many similarities,
Including our abilities.
Big, icy hearts.
We'll never drift apart.

As you read this poem,
I hope you get the theme.
This was never about Pluto,
It was always about me.

Teenage Ignorance

We met with the coordinator,
Who took my every wish.
Comparing all my choices,
For this once-in-a-lifetime trip.

I share the good news!
That I've been approved,
To fly across the world.
A check upon my bucket list.

Instead of a smile,
You frown.
Like I should be exiled.
As if this trip
Actually makes up,
For all of my stuff.

You forget that on my list
Was the erased wish
That I could be totally renewed,
Much more like you.

I wonder if given the choice,
You'd decide it'd be worth a rejoice,
To switch your life with mine.
Just to prove you could do it and shine.
After all, what is my suffering worth
If not, your reductive perspective of "a free trip"?

I look alright, right?

I look alright.
My chest is tight,
My mind is itching for a fight,
But at least I look alright.

I look alright.
My stomach pains,
My joints ache,
But at least I look alright.

I look alright.
I take more pills than I see light,
I've seen more scans with a slight,
But at least I look alright.

I look alright.
I have hidden scars that lace me,
And memories that taint me.
But at least I look alright.

I look alright.
That means the illness that mocks me is invisible,
So you can ignore my suffering and the indescribable.
Because I look alright, right?

I defy

47

I refused for life to be a waste.
I could never lose face.
Every minute filled,
With another goal I killed.

Each odd I defied,
Another stroke to my pride.
My teenage years,
I only allowed a few tears.

I didn't spend my nights
Rebelling against parental rights.
Instead of breaking ground rules,
I focused on my refuel.

Stored up enough,
To survive the hard stuff.
Each plausible defeat,
Felt like I'd succumbed to the Texas heat.

Losing to the statistics was my greatest fear.
Forcing my body to achieve like my peers.
Until my trained lungs shuttered,
And those clipped wings fluttered.

Mattie Paige

Bullshit from back then

I grew up jealous.
Incredibly overzealous.
Using my energy,
To fit into able-bodied legacies.

I got praised for making no complaints.
Pushing through my body's constraints.
My grades made up for my lacks.
All the while causing cracks.

My worth was set in my accomplishments.
I cried at minor admonishments.
In response, I promised to do better,
While ignoring the consuming pressure.

Requests so ridiculous,
Why did I never question it?
Once, I got told to stop coughing.
It silenced me so good, I felt my heart throbbing.

Begging for accommodations,
Fighting adults during negotiations.
Legally, I deserved it,
But minimal resources denied it.

Imagine, 90 degrees
No AC and a lung disease.
I could've sued.
But I hadn't wanted to pursue.

I couldn't push it,
For fear I would lose it.
I couldn't disrupt their perception of me,

For it would've meant the rejection of me.
I was the classic misunderstood teen,
With the misrepresented disease.
It was invisible,
So, I had to be invincible.

Didn't you used to be better?

What drove me,
Was the need to be,
Accepted.

To defy the odds.
That my body,
Should've lived up to.

I used to run,
On your,
Approval.

Now, even that,
Is not enough.
To push through.

You expect certainty.
Because I used to be.
But I've spiraled.

I'm not what I once was
Just like you,
We both progress.

My disease worsens,
Like your understanding.
My ability IS affected,

Even if you don't see it.

The Impact of A Wish

I owe a new perspective to my wish granters.
This idea that life has something to miss.
That a once-upon-a-daydream
Could become a dazzling reality,
Even with my impending mortality.

Those memories are more than just,
A cross-through on my bucket list.
Like the stamp on my passport,
They forever brand my heart.
A beautiful part of my story written,
Came a removal of prior inhibitions.

A flight to a new land?
They paid for the whole plan!
A tour through an ancient cathedral,
To look above Dublin,
From the view of an eagle.
I still remember how tranquil!

For this place full of history,
Made me excited to have a future.
That maybe what life I have,
Is worth living
Even with this sickness.

Claire Wineland

I first learned of Claire Wineland,
In my living room,
Doing my vest,
Elated to find her on tv,
Wearing it on her chest.
A person my age, living her life.
Winning an award,
For putting up a fight.
Even if Claire hadn't won those awards,
I still would've been impressed,
With all the strengths she possessed.
Candor, humor and wit,
How I love people,
Going through it.
She was the first I had seen
Living this belief,
That quality of life,
Is worth the dichotomy,
Of striving while you are dying.
I hadn't realized how important it was,
For CF people to share their voice,
But now that I hear her words
Ringing in my head,
Calling us to live,
I can say, "She inspired me to write this."

Claire Wineland.
Empowering the masses.
No matter what happens.

* A huge thank you to Claire's Place Foundation for their continuing support of the CF community and for the opportunity to include Claire in this collection.

Modulators

My genes created a melody,
By plugging mucus in my lungs,
To the rhythm of my heartbeat
And the bass of my tum.

The dominant wanted a ballad,
But the recessive won,
Thus a cacophony was born
At the hour I was.

Those discordant mutants,
Wrapped around like a sieve.
Affecting my whole piece,
Plucking chords from the minor D.

Until gene therapies joined the chorus,
A joyous uptick in tempo,
Burst a majestic symphony
With beautiful major keys.

Modulators regulate,
My body's harmony and hope
Making my life flow like a river,
My mucus no longer front and center.

I'm Just 18

I'm just an 18-year-old.
Trying to manage,
Cystic fibrosis.

I'm just an 18-year-old.
Trying to pack,
My vest.

I'm just an 18-year-old.
Trying to find,
A local pharmacy.

I'm just an 18-year old.
Meeting my new care team,
Feeling young and naive
For wanting a lollipop.

I'm just an 18-year-old.
Realizing this is a lot.
Thankful that I have a mom,
Who handled it all,
For so long,

And a dad.
Who worked hard,
To support my life.
All his own.

Part Three: The Reckoning of Adulthood

My day-to-day

I try to explain who I am day-to-day,
How my body feels and in what way.

Sometimes it's hard to say,
And today it's like a plague.

Like my mind suffered an earthquake,
And my bones only know how to ache.

Like the ligaments survived a flood,
And the sinews wish they could open up.

Like my muscles chased a tornado,
And my joints are only for show.

Like my sinuses are an active volcano,
And my lips will have to smile tomorrow.

The Pendulum

Tick-tock.
My grandfather clock.
Swings back and forth,
From disabled,
To healthily able.
I sway in between,
And I rarely fit the two extremes.

Tick-tock.
My grandfather clock.
Swings back and forth,
Energized to fatigued lies.
Positive to fear for life.
I'm abled enough to get by,
But disabled enough to cry.

Tick-tock.
My grandfather clock.
Takes up space in my living room
Imposing and aging.
Guests either ignore it,
Or complain of it's stature.
My friends admire my care for it.

Tick-tock.
My grandfather clock
Chimes every quarter hour,
Warning me of my waning power.
I count down the seconds of my day.
Waiting for the time to lay,
Only for you to say I should be okay.

Tick-tock.
My grandfather clock.
Is meant for me and me alone.
It shows I can finally read,
How my medicines affect me,
And my bodies changing abilities.

I used to remember

I used to remember what it felt like *before.*
Before the headaches began.
Before the realization that I was well and truly sick, forever.
Before I felt like a shell of who I could've been.

I used to be in the Math Honor Society. Salutatorian. A full-ride scholarship to college because I was labelled as 'smart'.

Now, trying to think through the fog that materializes in my synapses daily, I can hardly add two single-digit whole numbers without using my fingers.

I used to do sports. Powerlifting. Softball. I even got college offers that I didn't take because I wanted to pursue other interests that had felt feasible at the time.

Now, I could get a medal for getting out of bed, but it'd be a participation one because some days I lose that competition too.

I used to remember what it felt like to feel good. Physically. Mentally. Maybe even intrinsically.

What it felt like to have a head without the ache.
Lungs without the stuttering wheezing.
And life without the debilitating.

I still had the chronic illness. It's genetic, and I was born with it.
But it hadn't been debilitating.
I thought I had more time before my progressive disease, well, progressed.

Now, grief is my constant companion.

I hadn't even realized I could apply 'grief' to the losses of myself, and the opportunities I thought I had.

But the term feels right.

Because I used to remember what it felt like before.

Life Sentence...I mean Median Survival Age

The year was 2012. I was 11 years old. And I saw this pamphlet regarding a "median survival age". It had such a bright, radiant design. Baby blue background and sunflower yellow letters in a bubble letter font.

It distracted me from the life-altering information. From the big, mustard yellow THREE-SIX next to the words "median survival age of those with Cystic Fibrosis."

Did...did my parents know that they were older than my estimated age of survival?

Did my twin sister, with the same diagnosis, know that we might die before our future could happen?

Of course, medical professionals try to comfort you and your family by saying it's just an estimate. The middle number. Some people live longer.

The unspoken knowledge of how median estimates work haunts the quiet room.

Because some people don't make it to 36.

But doctors have to cope with their patient's life expectancies too.

When I found out the pamphlet had been true, it had felt like all my potential days were flung from that pamphlet back into my lungs, my gaze on the years that faded away.

All of my hard work,

Pills.

Doctors.

Intentionally reframing fears into joy because what other choice did I have?

All to *potentially* die before 40.

I'm still shaken, like the highest setting of my vest machine, the life sentence rattles around in me like my thick mucus.

I almost don't know what to do with the updated median survival that genetic modulators ascribed to us.

65.

We made it past 40.

I'm only to 25 years, but I'll keep going to the extent that I can control. Like the ways my body tries and tries every day of my life, I'll keep living. With my body.

Not in spite of, never in spite of.

We're a team.

And when my well-oiled, more like well-prescribed, God-given machine works with my carefully curated mental state, I feel good.

I feel like the median survival age isn't so suffocating.

I can finally look at that age estimate with a bit of psychological distance, thankfulness, and celebration.

Because we, the metaphoric lot of us living with CF, made it past 40.

And 50.

Even 60.

Maybe we'll make it so far, we won't have to keep track of our median survival age.

Rare

I'd like to be rare,
Like a ruby.
Glittering red,
And tougher than steel.

Durable and stable.
Something,
Others sought after.
Rare enough to give their all too.

I'm rare.
Like a disease.
Gilding interest,
For being an unsolved case.

Everchanging.
And frustrating.
Thought of as complicated,
Not worth effort past the initial fascination.

Mattie Paige

Erosion

I am a granite rock.
Perched along an ancient valley.
Grey and arching high.
Ready for the light to hit my edges.

I am a granite rock.
Awaiting the great flood,
By water from above,
Turning me into sludge.

I am a granite rock.
Feeling the wind,
Whip me apart,
Depositing me too far.

I am granite rock.
Getting split apart,
By glacial art,
Carving out my spot.

My body is a granite rock.
My disease erodes,
Progressing my boulders,
Into flattened pebbles.

Schemes

When something big happens,
It's met with empathy,
And all these,
Caring schemes.
But what about my day-to-day?
The way I always ache.
Would you meet me,
With a gentleness
That wouldn't just take.
Would you caress my face
And wipe my tears,
Even though you know,
This is my every day?

GOOD OLE DR. SHITE

Good ole Dr. Shite.
Chose this profession,
Out of spite.

Good ole Dr. Shite.
Always thinks,
He's right.

Good ole Dr. Shite.
Wants to run some scans
Because of my fright.

Good ole Dr. Shite.
Said it can't be,
It's just my plight.

Good ole Dr. Shite.
Diagnosed with no empathy.
Constantly feeding me slights.

Good ole Dr. Shite.
Relies on old evidence,
To treat my modern fight.

Good ole Dr. Shite.
Tries his best,
While waiting for the re-ignite.

The Mirrored Knight

Knighthood has been bestowed
When a commoner hits a crossroad.
An unexpected quest,
Hoping for progress.

A noble warrior,
Armored in looking glass.
Wielding a sword,
Bracing with a shield.

The Mirrored Knight
Doesn't value stealth,
But spends it's days
Fighting both friend and foe,
For a drop of wealth
In the form of good health.

The Mirrored Knight
Tries to be perceived,
The way the knight needs,
But all people ever see
Is themselves
Looking back at thee.

The knight slashes
The double-edged sword,
Goading for a score
Only to get ignored.

The knight moves,
Behind the shield
Trying to yield
But fate has been sealed.

Mattie Paige

The person under the helm,
Is actually in another realm.
Self-advocating for deserved care,
Unsure how to be helped.

YOLO

They say to live
Like you are dying
But that's all I've ever done

Death is Coming

We have limited days.
We have bodies that try.
We have thoughts to dissect the why.

We find ways
To survive society,
No matter the impropriety.

We go through tragedy,
In various forms.
For some it's the norm.

I'm not sure how I got here,
Reveling in this morbid comfort.
It was a last-ditch effort,
To cope with humanity's impending fate...

Death is coming for us all,
No matter how we stall.

Stuck

I'm continually stuck.
Between not wanting to suffer
Through medical abhorrences,
And being unable to choose
The only other alternative.

So, I cry in bed again.
Before I always decide,
To give life another try.

Part 4: The Acceptance Aftermath

A Tough Pill to Swallow (but we've trained for it)

What a time to live,
With Cystic Fibrosis.
Modulators and
Representation
How I wish,
The elders could've had this.

Young enough to benefit,
But old enough to remember,
The thirty-year median survival,
The new drug trials,
Those who died,
I honor.

The hardest pill to swallow,
Is that I'm gifted modern medicine,
Yet my disease is still polluting me.
The advancements are a step forward--
Not yet a step out,
Still, a piece of hope
In this continual fight.

Decoy

Maybe it's not me,
And my rare disease,
Maybe it's other people,
Needing a dose of reality.

I went into this meeting
Expecting the same results,
But you didn't even question
My diagnoses' interventions.

What a breath of fresh air,
To be totally seen.
Without having to make a scene,
No need to indulge in obscenities.

While it's sad that I'm shocked,
That I haven't been mocked,
I cry tears of joy,
Your inclusivity wasn't a decoy.

Other Bodies I'd Want

If all the bodies of the world,
Lined up for the taking,
I'd trek around the globe
To stand in front of my own.

(I'm not sure that's true, but I want it to be)

Being Real

I always feel this pressure.
To be grateful and inspiring.
And it's not that I'm not thankful,
And I can't control if people...
Find me stereotypically inspiring.
But it's the notion
That society
Can control how disabled people
Feel, think and behave.
I already have one thing
Doing it's best to control me.
Like puppet strings
Attached to my organs.
I don't need another
Unachievable expectation
Pulling at my head and heart.

Let me be real.
Let me be mournful and wretched.
Let me be joyful and lively.
Even neutral.

Let me be all things,
In my own time.
Don't make me be only positive,
Just because it makes you more comfortable.

Spirituality

It would be dishonorable
To not mention the tabernacle.
This mystical idea of hope
That my life is not only a negative slope.
The Good News truly helps me cope.

My life on earth is a never-ending battle,
Of wit, health and what matters.
A fight until earthbound death,
But what if that wasn't the end?

What if there was a second chance,
Filled with joy, laughter and existence?
A powerful God of comfort,
Gifting a place where my lungs won't ache.

Each wheezing breath,
No longer a doomed circumstance.
No use for my pills, vials or trials,
I will have survived the volatile.

My thorn is no longer worthless,
For I have hope in the name of Jesus.
This suffering will one day end,
But until then,
I will do my best,
With this illness.

Mercies

What small mercies
O' Lord, have you given me.
That my medications work,
That my loved ones gather around,
That I am still able to seek your face,
In the despair of my mind.

What small mercies,
Add to the fullness of my life.
To the joy I clutch onto,
To the breath in my lungs,
As I sing your praises.

These small mercies,
Drip your glory,
Like honey flowing,
I drink.
I taste.
I know,
That the Lord is good.

Proclaim

I have Cystic Fibrosis,
And it's time I proclaim it.
I am life-threateningly,
progressively,
and chronically ill,

And ready for life's fill.

Life is mine for the taking,
Though sometimes it feels like it took me.

a rarity

A Fraction

I like to think,
About my own strengths
Without regards
To others' perspectives.

Except my therapist.
I pay her good money
To break through
My one-track mind.

It's usually always,
Bad, bad, bad.
Because brains are wired
To remember the sad.

But my therapist,
Is allowed to push,
My psyche
To be objective.

To grasp onto the whispers
That maybe I have,
Something good to live for,
That maybe even *I am good...*

That maybe,
This illness made me,
Flexible
And empathetic.

That maybe
I persist.
Because

I care.
About others.
And myself.
Despite how much,
I deny it.

Yet, a part of me still wonders,
Could I have been all of those things,
All on my own?
It's not my disease,
But really just me.

This is all a part of a whole,
The disease, my character.
They are not dependent on each other.
But are two concepts floating by,
Occasionally intermingling.

Sentiments

People always ask why I write such sad things,
But when I gave them the poem,
I was smiling.
The words were neutral.
The poem wasn't drenched in my despair, agony or rage.
It just was.

And it made me realize,
Their 'sad experiences' are my usual.
My circumstances aren't sad to me anymore.
Maybe it's desensitization.
Maybe it's the acceptance that isn't as far out of reach as I
thought.

My life isn't sad.
It took me a while to be able to say that.
To feel that way.
But it's just my life.
I'm tired of feeling like their perception of my life is important.

I want to be bold.
To just live without wondering how other people will react,

When I say I take pills every day and with every meal,
When I tell them my liver function is elevated again,
When I explain the pain I feel *all the time.*

It's hard sometimes.
I feel sad sometimes.
But,
I like my life.
Pills and pain included. Or despite.
Still deciphering that line of thought.

But I like who I'm becoming.

I go through hard things, but,
I handle it.
I cope.
Yet, I still receive, "I'm sorry" and "Hope you get better".

I understand the sentiment.
I appreciate the goodwill.
But my disease is something I've lived with since birth.
It's not new or novel.
So, the well wishes don't really...
Punctuate through me, anymore.

They used to.
But now, the one who spoke them to me, can keep them.
Cast them into the air.
Will them towards me with every good intention.
But it means more for them, than me.

I don't need a stranger's sentiments anymore.

But the stranger does.

But I like who I'm becoming.

The Power of Sisters

I think of memories visually, audibly and emotionally. Like a film reel rolling through my head, with my sister the shining star.

She's been present for so much of my story. She's experienced *basically* the same things I did. CF. Enzymes. PFTs. Quarterly checkups. Coughing. Insipid adolescent comments. Transitioning to adult care. Orkambi, then Trikafta.

She's seen it all. She's felt it all, alongside me.

And there's one recurring memory I relive often, a thousand different ways with her. It's one of the best parts of my film reel...

It's Friday night after the day of high school classes, and the freedom that comes with no school for two days is bubbling up. I finish my vest and nebulizer treatments, the quiet after turning off the buzzing machines searing my mind.

Ah. I've finished another round of being responsible.

I sneak to the darkened kitchen, using the left-on light from my bedroom to illuminate the path to our stainless steel fridge.

I open the double doors, the bright LED fridge light shining on the food I set out to gather. It's stockpiled into my hands, haphazardly balancing as I grin.

Cheese dip, salsa, chocolate pudding, waters.

Then, I trek to the dark pantry, not even needing to turn on its light to grab the tortilla chips and plastic spoons.

I practically skipped to my sister's room, excited for our weekly, late-night escapade. My parents are asleep across the hall, no idea that we do this every Friday.

Right as I creak her wooden door open, she snaps off her nebulizer, beaming as she unbuckles her pink vest and throws it on the floor carelessly.

She clears the comforter from her bed as I set down our array of fattening foods. If you didn't know, people with CF grew up being told to overeat because we wouldn't absorb half the nutrients anyways. As teenagers, we consumed food as if we were hungry whirlpools, pulling anything delicious into our stomachs.

So, we laid it all out, not even worried about crumbs in bed. Blasphemous, I know. But, for once, we weren't worried about anything.

The yellow lights of the bedroom fall around us as animals chitter outside in the night. We start out whispering as we snack on our feast, the saltiness from the chips just what the doctor ordered.

Eventually, our whispers turn into raucous laughs while falling over, as joyous, ridiculous tears stream down our cheeks.

We laugh so much, it turns into coughs as we reach for our waters.

And I love it.

We understand life with CF together, and we thrive, together.

Every moment with her proves that rareness is a double-edged sword we've been taught to wield.

The weapon isn't as heavy when we hold it together.

Our Lungs Might Fail, but Our CF Voices Never Will

It was 2020, and I was so, *so* alone.

We had just been sent home from our second semester of college because of the brewing pandemic.

And my doctors recommended that I, and people like me, the *blasted* (satirical) immunocompromised, should quarantine until a vaccine came out.

That we should shelter in place.

Wipe down our groceries.

Increase our Vitamin D.

Order prescriptions before the shortages start.

Wear N95 masks...

And it's funny, because out of all these rules and regulations, the masks weren't a big change to our routine, though the world acted like it was. Most of us with CF already knew the benefits of face coverings, because we had been doing it since we were children.

Every time we went to the doctor's office.

Every time we were in close quarters with other CF'ers.

Since my birth, I was told to social distance from anyone bearing similar genetics. Anyone with our rare disease was someone we kept *past* arm's length. The infamous six-feet-apart.

It took the vaccine a year to come out for my location. Which meant a year without face-to-face contact, with *anyone*. Not just other CF'ers.

A year of online schooling, social demise, doomscrolling and whipped coffee (yes, I fell into that glorious trap.)

My sleep schedule was non-existent. I purposefully stayed up till 4am, just because there was nothing else to do.

The morning would still come, and we would still be on lockdown.

People would still talk shit online, and I would still be angry about it.

Eventually, I turned to drawing when my fingers found an old charcoal pencil and sketchpad. I drew people, places and my first poems.

I wrote down the conversations I wanted to have when I saw my friends again, *in person.* I jotted down memories I wanted to make in the future, *in person.* When the longing got to be destructive, I would...

Cue the beloved doomscrolling.

The trending audios.

The celebrity podcasts.

The tragic videos.

Then one day, a square photo caused a blip in the recurrent, depressing monotony that had become my "new normal".

Without even saying anything, this woman in the photo held my attention. She had my hope fuming from her nebulizer as it curled up into the air towards her face.

I followed her immediately.

Back then, that was the only form of new social connection I had, so I scrolled, and scrolled, through her social media page.

Lo-and-behold, a vest machine.

The woman had CF.

And she had created a server for people with CF to join while we were on lockdown.

I messaged her, though my heart was racing. And she added me into the chat with a smiley face and an introduction.

Flash forward to 2026, I'm still in that group chat, but now, there's almost 100 of us in this niche corner of the world. We're from different places, different experiences but we bear the same general diagnosis.

But that's not all.

a rarity

We understand each other.

I can send words like:

>Liver Enzymes
>
>Alyftrek
>
>And "how to keep a job when you're fucking exhausted but affordable health insurance is tied to your employment status?"

And they get it.

They give advice.

They validate feelings and fears.

They remind me of my power. (I hope I do the same for them.)

All because of one person's voice.

One person helped me survive the worst year of my life by providing an escape rooted in shared realities.

One person gave a group of rarities a place to be together, unrestricted by society.

And as I look back on that first year of this group, I realize how strong we really are.

There were people waiting and waiting for this promised vaccine that was supposed to release us from the shackles of COVID-19 (and 20, 21, 22...).

People pleading for others to understand why masks were so important (or even if you didn't care to wear one, that you still cared about us, the *blasted* (satirical) immunocompromised.)

And through all of that, we adhered to our medical routines while the world felt like it crumbled around us.

We were so unwavering.

Determined.

Angry.

Fatigued.

Hungry for life.

And we still are.

And we won't be silent.

Quality Over Quantity

Would you rather have,
A thousand cups of mediocre coffee
Or one just the right shade?

Would you prefer,
Hundreds of books you'd never choose
Or one made just for you?

Would you like,
Tens of bouquets of flowers
Or one given by someone you love?

Would you want to spend your days,
Living the life of another,
Or have one to live your way?

While quantity is a hopeful expectation,
It's never a guarantee.
One day you'll have the revelation,
That without quality,
Quantity is only a fabrication.

Mattie Paige

What is Unconditional Love?

It's a stroke of a thumb on my hair,
As I lay on your thigh
And on the heating pad.

It's a done-deal chore,
With acknowledgement
Of my limited energy levels.

It's soft encouragement,
To keep up with my pills
When I really, *really* don't want to.

It's loyalty in the form,
Of rage on my behalf
When anyone dismisses my needs.

It's the celebration,
When a day comes with
everything working.
The doctors,
The medicines,
The insurance,
My acceptance,
Their joy,

It all comes together to create a beautiful reminder of why I'm
prioritizing the steps to my survival.
This, *you*, are one of the reasons I want to live!
You make me feel alive!
Unconditional love is any person that makes the pain of
surviving another day worth it.

Aging, not like milk or wine, just aging.

When did my youthful freckles,
Turn into age spots I crave.
The way they tan in the sun,
After I've persisted another day.
How they wrinkle and stay,
What a privilege it is to age.

Thankful

I am so thankful.
For each breath.
That flutters
Into my chest.
Each huff,
That doesn't cause
A cough up.

I am so thankful.
For each medicine,
The researchers propose
And the subjects that allow
Their existence to be studied
To give the masses,
A glimpse at an improved body.

I am so thankful.
For the loved ones
That are always there.
Through hours of,
A hospital timeshare.

I am so thankful.
For my providers,
That do their best.
To understand a disease,
They will never live with.

I am so thankful.
For my resilience.
To keep living,
With my many
Bodily horrors.

I am so thankful.
For the gift of life.
To experience,
Darkness and light.

I am so thankful.
For the joys,
I create.

I am so thankful.
For words upon a page.

I am so thankful.

a rarity

The more I think about my life,
The more I realize,
How rare it is.
Rare like a ruby,
and a disease.
To inhale.
Exhale.
And to do it again.

To take the body we were dealt,
And live the life it insists.
Yet, I still glimpse a flicker of potential.
The potential to live.
Maybe, not well.
Maybe, not long.
Maybe, hardly at all.

But it's there...
In the quiet room with hot beverages, yellow twinkling lights and
comfort.
In the adrenaline-rushed space with pulsing yells, roaring ears
and euphoria.
Even in the hospital room, with a tumbling stomach, pricking
eyes and inescapable defeat.

Life is everywhere.
Even in you.
Especially, in you.
When you cough and cry and almost die.
Especially when you laugh and smile and dance for a while.

What a rarity it is to be,
You.
And even Me.

Acknowledgements

I loved writing this book. While it brought up memories of the dark kind, it felt so invigorating to face them and put them to use. I felt emboldened to end this poetic journey the way I did. With acceptance of my many outlooks on life and abilities. I hadn't expected to end on a positive note because this book was born when I was filled with rage and desperation.

I wanted people to understand what it was like to live with a life-threatening, progressive chronic illness. I wanted people to know why I have to prioritize my health to the extent that I do. I wanted people to know that if I failed them because of the ways my body functions, that it isn't my fault. It just is. And I felt so out of place because it felt like so few people understood.

I realized that I didn't often challenge their perspectives by sharing my reality and rareness. I let them live with their limited understanding of who I am and allowed them to make decisions that directly affected me and my health. This book is my breaking free. It's my shout into the void that I matter. That I've always mattered. And that people like me matter. That our voices and lives behind the scene affect the things out in the open.

If you are reading this, I want you to know that I am not trying to pressure you into sharing what you aren't comfortable with, but that for me, I was put on earth to encourage. The kind of encouragement that acknowledges both pain and joy. The kind that weeps when others weep and rejoice when others rejoice.

I hope as you read this, we wept and rejoiced together. I hope it encourages you to keep living whatever life you were given. And for all of us with a rare disease, I pray you leave these pages with the hope that someone will see your rareness and admire it. The rareness in you that's like a ruby and a disease.

So, my first acknowledgement is to you, dear reader. Thank you for your time, consideration and anything else you offered to me when reading my work. It truly means the world. You have seen my rareness, and for that I am so, so thankful.

Secondly, I want to thank my sister. You are such a light in the darkness. You make me feel seen. Not just because we share a disease, but because we recognize the rubies in each other. Thank you for ranting and raving with me. I love telling you my every book idea while you patiently wait for them to come out, ha! Thank you for your endless support.

To my husband, you are so fiercely loyal and uplifting. I appreciate how we've built our lives together and how you handle coping with a disease I had my whole life to get used to. Thank you for helping me live the life I've longed for.

To my parents, for caring for me my entire life. For encouraging me and reminding me to keep living. I love you both so much.

To my doctors, for caring for me even when I get tired of it. For trying, harder than most, to understand a disease you don't live with. I wouldn't be where I am without you. Thank you so, so much.

To Make-A-Wish, The CF Foundation, The Boomer Esiason Foundation, Claire's Place Foundation, and any other foundations that continue to value the lives of those living with CF. Thank you for your dedication to our community.

Finally, thank you to my beta readers and my writing group for supporting me. I would not be the writer I am today without all of you! You make life sparkle and help me describe the way it does. I'm excited to keep yapping and writing with you all!

With love and a handful of pills,

Mattie

a rarity

Reviews

If you would like to leave a review, feel free to write your thoughts down on Goodreads, Amazon, or social media! Reviews are greatly appreciated and a fabulous way to help out indie authors, such as myself!

About The Author

Mattie Paige is a multi-genre author that enjoys writing the vast array of emotions humans feel. She has a BS in Psychology and currently spends her days writing on the side. Other pieces centering around her chronic illness includes, "Laundry Makes Me Think of My Mom" in FLARE Magazine, and "My Good Friend, Death" in Wishbone Literary Magazine, coming in the spring of 2026. Mattie's debut poetry book, "The Woman, The Love, The Death" can be found where you buy books! When not living her introverted dream at home with her husband and dog, she can be found yearning for an iced coffee and reading romance novels.

Want to stay up to date with Mattie and her future projects? Feel free to follow her on social media (@authormattiepaige) or subscribe to her newsletter, "Mattie Paige's Insider Info" via Substack.

www.ingramcontent.com/pod-product-compliance
Lightning Source LLC
Chambersburg PA
CBHW041333120726
48005CB00014B/2228